Mom
I love you

This book belongs to

_____

Published by:
Modus Vivendi Publishing Inc.
3859 Laurentian Autoroute
Laval, Quebec
Canada H7L 3H7

Cover and inside page design: Marc Alain

Translation by: Catherine Lavoie

Picture Credits: © SuperStock and Image Club

Legal Deposit: 1ˢᵗ Quarter 2001
National Library of Canada

Canadian Cataloguing in Publication Data
Desbois, Hervé
    Mom I love you
    (Heartfelt Series)
    Translation of: Maman je t'aime.
    ISBN: 2-89523-057-9
    1. Mothers. 2. Mothers - Pictorial works.
    I. Title. II. Series.
HQ759.D4713 2001   306.874'3   C00-942050-9

Canadä We acknowledge the financial support of the Government
of Canada through the Book Publishing Industry Development
Program (BPIDP) for our publishing activities.

Mom
I love you

HERVÉ DESBOIS

MV PUBLISHING

"A mother is the truest friend we have,
when trials, heavy and sudden, fall upon us (...)
still will she cling to us, and endeavour
by her kind precepts and counsels
to dissipate the clouds of darkness,
and cause peace to return to our hearts."

Washington Irving (1783-1859)

Whoever we are and whatever we are in this world, we are each a woman's child. And no matter the kind of relationship we now have with her, she will always hold a special place in our life. Perhaps she has now become a friend, a confidante, a counsellor? Or maybe the circumstances have, one way or another, made us wander far from one another; or perhaps she is now no more than a fleeting memory that life has left us? No matter what paths are followed or what goals are pursued, what directions and choices keep us apart or bring us together, somewhere deep inside each of us, there is this first love, this first contact with life. I often hear people say we owe life to our mothers. But what do they have to say, those mothers from here and everywhere? Ask your own mother; maybe will she answer that life was simply a gift from her to you.

For a Mother

I asked so much of you
And never really knew
The reason for the shadows in your eyes
The meaning of your silent sighs

Often my insolence
Was only matched by your patience
I crossed all the borders
But your love never faltered

And all those silent nights
You spent 'til morning light
Sitting next to my bed
Caressing my forehead

You would have pushed my fever away
Had you only known the way
But your soothing made the pain flee
As you stayed so close to me

But the child's heart beating in my chest
Never gave you a moment's rest
I was blind and free of all concerns
Withholding the words you had so earned

> "A mother is a mother still,
> The holiest thing alive"

Samuel Taylor Coleridge (1772-1834)

I had been watching her walk back and forth in the house for hours. Despite my young age, I was capable of understanding certain things, probably more than adults could imagine! I could sense quite clearly that she wasn't in her normal state. Sometimes our eyes met, but so briefly... as if she didn't want to leave me enough time to read in her eyes and know what was going on inside of her. But I knew very well that something was wrong... I knew without really knowing or rather, I had the perception of some ongoing event, for all that I couldn't explain it.

I could, however, feel her nervousness grow and above all rub off on me as the day went by! Of course, I didn't like to see her in that state, but what could I do about it? Suddenly, the Superman I was in my dreams and in my games, the dispenser of justice who fought against sorrow and distress and in whom I believed with all my might was

(...)

becoming insipid and useless. The magic force that inhabited my child's life was all of a sudden blown to pieces, replaced by a feeling of total helplessness as the worst of ineptitudes.

That is where my thoughts had led me when I heard some sort of high-pitched moan, like an ultimate call for help that came too late. I rushed over to the bathroom from where the sound seemed to come. And I stood frozen in the doorway. She was there, lying on the floor over a bundle of old blankets, looking at me with her big eyes that seemed to be asking for help, eyes where astonishment and incomprehension could be found.
- "Don't worry, everything will be fine. It's her first litter, after all,"
Then my cat gave out a long mewing, just as the first kitten came out of her womb.

Matriarchy is defined as a system of social organization in which descent and inheritance are traced through the female line. (Ref. *Webster's*)

❧

According to different studies on ancient matriarchal societies, mothers didn't use their powers to impose domination on others, unlike patriarchy, where men fully exercise domination!

❧

Some of Brittany's localities have had a "matriarchal society". Because of the deep-sea fishing, which saw men leaving for six to eight months of the year, village life depended on women. Moreover, girls chose their "suitors" and, once married, kept their maiden names. Alone for most of the year, they took charge of family life, and those families were often very large!

Matriarchal organization, found in some nations in antiquity, seems to have found its origin in the mystery that procreation represented then, giving women the status of "co-creators" of the world.

Some of Vietnam's peoples still observe certain rites linked to matriarchy. A girl has the right to choose her husband; and after the wedding, the young man has to go live with his wife's family.

But it is in China's south-east mountains that one of the last traditional societies dominated by women lives on: the Mosu people have kept their matriarchal social organization in spite of everything.

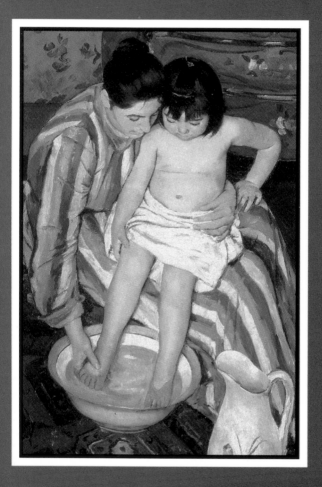

"A father's love is higher than the mountain.
A mother's love is deeper than the ocean."

Japanese proverb

"Begin, baby boy, to recognize
your mother with a smile."

Virgil (70-19 B.C.)

"A man loves his sweetheart the most,
his wife the best, but his mother the longest."

Irish proverb

"The heart of a mother is a deep abyss
at the bottom of which you will always
find forgiveness."

Honoré de Balzac ((1799-1850)

"Life began with waking up
and loving my mother's face."

George Eliot (1819-1880)

Memories

An old faded picture
Where life seems frozen
A moment of happiness
That was before, that was elsewhere

Those unmoving faces
Calmly gazing at me
From the other side of time
Speak of another time

From the other side of the mirror
They tell their story
It's a silent story
That writes itself in my head

Fleeting characters
Familiar faces
I am reunited with the past
It was yesterday, I remember

And I am there
With my brothers, so little
And that smiling face
It's her, my mother.

> "A mother remains a mother,
> no matter what child weeps before her."

H. D.

Who has not, one day, been proud of his or her mother? Personally, I don't have to look very far to find one of those moments. A moment as dramatic as it was exceptional. We were on our summer vacation in a typical family hotel. It was very simple wherever we went in the hotel, we were sure to find children. There were some of all ages, even babies. Confident in my eight years of age, I myself was part of the "short trousers' tourist community".

That day, it was raining. The playroom was therefore busy with noisy and lively activities on the adults' as well as on the children's part. In the middle of this happy hubbub, a tiny baby was sleeping in his Moses basket. His parents were taking advantage of his nap to play cards, and no one seemed to be paying attention to the baby, not even me and yet I was playing right next to him.

At one point, his mother left the card table and went close to the basket to make sure everything was all right. And in a fraction of a second, everything changed. Lightning landing right in the middle of the group wouldn't have had a more striking effect: the baby's mother had just let out the most heartrending cry I had ever heard. She was there, trembling next to the basket, clasping in her arms

(...)

the lifeless body of her baby. Her husband, panic-stricken, ran towards her, but neither one nor the other seemed able to react adequately. All of a sudden, coming from nowhere, I saw my mother run towards the couple, grasp the child and without a word, lay him down on the table where I was playing. Everybody was in such a state of shock that no one asked a single question. Mommy was trained in first-aid and, with fast and steady movements, she positioned the baby in order to give him mouth-to-mouth resuscitation. The mother's sobs, which she was having great difficulty keeping in check, seemed to intensify the overwhelming silence. Everybody looked as if they were holding their breath, like a desperate effort to pass this breath on to the poor infant. Tirelessly, mommy was repeating the same movements, breathing life into the Life sleeping inside that frail little body. The resuscitation manoeuvres seemed to last forever. Then, suddenly, the baby gasped and my mother rapidly turned him over on his side. I made a face seeing the baby vomit, but mommy smiled.
-"He's coming back..."
And no one could keep from smiling when the baby started crying. Mommy had just given life, once again.

Mothers of the World

Whether she's white, black, Christian or Muslim, a mother is a mother. No matter the origins, the culture or the religion, maternal love seems to transcend human laws: it is universal.

A mother's tears have the same transparency and the same taste, no matter where on earth they were shed. And the smiles, the warmth, as if this love went beyond the human frontiers of race and culture. A universal love that digs its roots and draws its strength from somewhere else than the material world. Somewhere else, in the depths of the human soul, in the timeless universe of the spirit which knows only the colour of love and the language of feelings.

In spite of the evolution of roles in modern society, I keep the image, maybe a little obsolete, of the nursing mother. Traditionally, isn't that one of the first contacts, favoured if ever there was one, the mother breast-feeding her child? I know the cliché cannot please everyone but it doesn't matter. My mother cooking, that was something!

Hidden Treasures

For four treasures, you will need:
- 4 brioches
- 4 eggs (preferably small)
- 30 g/1oz butter
- Grated cheese
- Salt and pepper

Cut the "heads" of the brioches and butter them. Then dig out the insides of the brioches, being careful not to make a hole in the crust. Butter the inside surfaces and put the brioches in the oven at around 125º C/250º F for five minutes (check to make sure they don't burn!). Take them out of the oven and break an egg in each one. Sprinkle with salt and pepper, add a little grated cheese and put them back in the oven at 180º C/350º F with their "heads" but without covering them, until the egg whites harden, about ten minutes. Serve the brioches covered with their "heads". Irresistible...

"Every mother's child is handsome."

German proverb

"The supreme happiness of life
is the conviction that we are loved."

Victor Hugo (1802-1885)

"Heaven is at the feet of mothers."

Persian proverb

"All I am I owe to my mother."

George Washington (1732-1799)

"A loving heart is the truest wisdom."

Charles Dickens (1812-1870)

A Mother

A mother is...
Open arms
Outstretched hands
Love in its purest form

An immense heart
That knows no bounds
To love and teach
To give due praise

Eyes to see
When shadows lurk
And ears to hear
When pain holds fast

Words needed
To right the wrongs
To stop the hates
And rekindle the smiles

A mother is...
The sun that rises
The night that ends
The gift of life.

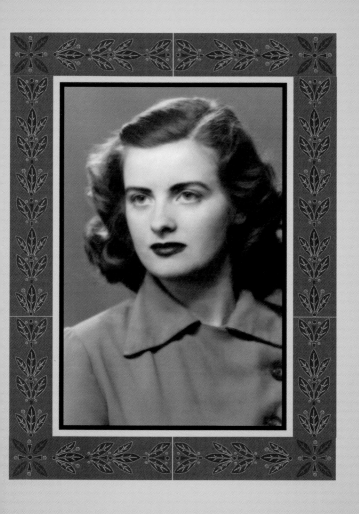

"The safest shelter is a mother's breast."

Jean-Pierre Claris de Florian

Life is full of meetings, sometimes incredible. It was in July of 1973, I was hitch-hiking through Europe, looking for adventure. As it sometimes happens with that mode of transportation, I found myself with a "breakdown", in a little village in Bavaria. Night had started to fall and I was still far from the city where, according to my plans, I should have spent the night in a youth hostel.
Steadfast in the face of adversity, I finally decided to ask the parish priest for hospitality. I first became concerned when I didn't see any steeple in the surroundings. And with darkness coming down, I had some trouble finding my bearings. I therefore decided to use my "schoolish and ap-proximate" German to ask the first passer-by the way to the presbytery. The first person I approach-ed was a woman. She looked at me inquisitively and wanted to know why I was asking. Short of words, I simply answered: to sleep. Suddenly I realized my appearance was certainly something to be frightened of, me, a young bearded stranger, hairy, lost in the middle of the country with a back-pack as sole baggage. She stared at me for an instant and I almost went on my own way for fear of sudden-ly hearing her scream for help. But no. She had a little smile and simply asked me to follow her.

(...)

I thought I was in luck, telling myself she would lead me directly to the presbytery. My confidence was starting to waver seeing the maze of streets we were following. But to my surprise, she suddenly headed for a residence that looked nothing like a presbytery! I stopped on the sidewalk, puzzled, but the woman motioned me to follow her. She opened the door and showed me in... to her own house!

Then I didn't get a chance to say much. Without even asking me anything, she gave me food, got me settled in a guest room, then she introduced me to her family... in pictures. With hand gestures and slowly repeated words, she made me understand that her husband was a travelling salesman and that she had two children. She showed me a young man in a picture and pointed at me. Seeing my confused look, she explained to me slowly, choosing her words carefully so I would understand. Here is approximately what she told me: "My son is your age and is hitch-hiking right now, like you. And I'm worried about him, just like your mother must be worried about you. So I welcomed you just as I would like him to be welcomed wherever he goes."

Mother, from the Latin mater, which means "woman who has given birth to a child," is a word that through time has expanded and become richer, taking on the notion of provider, of the maternal figure, of the one who takes care of others. It is a word found in fact in many expressions to indicate the generating principle, the origin, etc. It is therefore a word that is full of meaning in the imagination of humanity. So when I hear some scientists reducing human beings to machines, I can't help but pull a face. The love of a mother certainly goes beyond all the laws of physics, chemistry and biology. Those scientists who try to explain Life have certainly forgotten the essentials!

Fertile Mothers...

The fertility record belongs to two women.
Mrs Fiodor Vassiliev, a Russian who lived from 1707 to 1782 had sixty-nine children in twenty-seven pregnancies: quadruplets four times, triplets seven times and twins sixteen times.
Mrs Bernard Scheinber, an Austrian who died in 1011 at the age of fifty-six, also had sixty-nine children. Her husband remarried and had eighteen children with his second wife!
Closer to us, in 1989, Maria Olivera gave birth to her thirty-second child when she was fifty years old.

(...)

In France, Madeleine Davaud, born in 1910, had twenty-five children between 1928 and 1958.
In 1946, a Brazilian woman had ten children from one pregnancy: two boys and eight girls.

(Ref. *Quid 2000*)

Tips from Yesterday's Mothers

Salt makes milk turn sour. Therefore, when preparing porridge or sauces, it is better to add it only at the end of the preparation.
Boiling water takes out most fruit stains. Pour the boiling water over the stain as you would through a sieve so you don't get the material wetter than necessary.
Tomato juice takes out ink and rust stains from clothing and hands.
A tablespoonful of turpentine, added to the wash, is a powerful help in whitening clothes.
Petroleum softens the leather of shoes hardened by humidity and makes it as flexible and soft as when it was new. Not to be done too often or the leather could get ruined.
Cold rainwater and a little soda takes grease out of all washable materials.

"A father may turn his back on his child,
brothers and sisters may become
inveterate enemies, husbands may desert
their wives, wives their husbands.
But a mother's love endures through all."

Washington Irving (1783-1859)

"When eating fruit,
think of the person who planted the tree."

Vietnamese proverb

"So much of what we know we learn at home."

Unknown

"Who ran to help me when I fell,
And would some pretty story tell,
Or kiss the place and make it well?
My Mother."

Ann Taylor (1782-1866)

"He that would the daughter win,
Must with the mother first begin."

English proverb

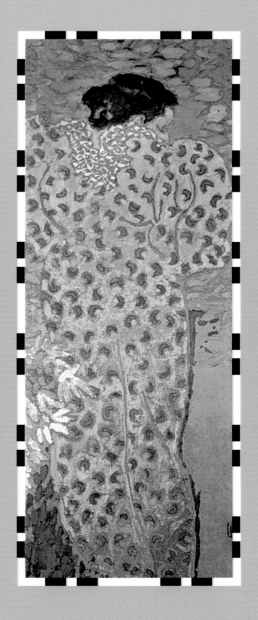

What You Gave Me

My life began
With your love for me
I was your plan
For all to see

Tiny hands you held
When you hushed me to sleep
Tenderness I felt
With my every heartbeat

As I grew older
And went my own way
Our opinions would differ
But your love did not sway

You taught me well
I never forgot
Even when I fell
Give up I would not

What you gave me
Was more than you thought
And now all can see
And now all will know
What you mean to me
How I love you so.

"The mother's yearning, that completest
type of the life in another life
which is the essence of real human love,
feels the presence of the cherished child
even in the debased, degraded man."

George Eliot (1819-1880)

"A mother's children are like dreams.
None are as wonderful as hers."

Chinese proverb

"So for the mother's sake the child was dear
And dearer was the mother for the child"

Samuel Taylor Coleridge (1772-1834)

"The consciousness of loving and being loved
brings a warmth and richness to life
that nothing else can bring."

Oscar Wilde (1854-1900)

"God could not be everywhere
and so he made mothers."

Jewish proverb

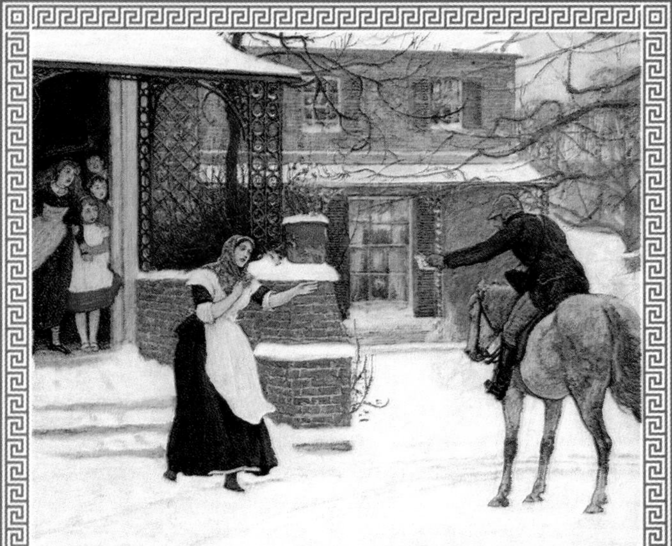